BECOME A VEHICLE MECHANIC

Car Maintenance, Bike Repair & More

Ashley Kuehl

Abdo & Daughters
MIDDLE GRADE NONFICTION
An imprint of Abdo Publishing
abdobooks.com

ABDOBOOKS.COM

Published by Abdo Publishing, a division of ABDO, PO Box 398166, Minneapolis, Minnesota 55439. Copyright © 2025 by Abdo Consulting Group, Inc. International copyrights reserved in all countries. No part of this book may be reproduced in any form without written permission from the publisher. Abdo & Daughters™ is a trademark and logo of Abdo Publishing.

Printed in the United States of America, North Mankato, Minnesota
102024
012025

THIS BOOK CONTAINS RECYCLED MATERIALS

Design: Denise Hamernik, Mighty Media, Inc.
Production: Mighty Media, Inc.
Editor: Katherine Chu

Cover Photographs: Adobe Stock (air filter, engine, fuel filter); Shutterstock Images (gas can, gears, jumper cables, oil, repair shop background, spark plug, start/stop button, steering column, taillights, wrenches, wheel)

Interior Photographs: Adobe Stock, p. 36, 37 (left), 42-43 (bottom), 57; dave_7/Flickr, p. 9; Gun Powder Ma/Wikimedia Commons, p. 6 (bottom); Mighty Media, Inc. (project photos), pp. 50, 51; Shutterstock Images, pp. 3, 4, 5 (all), 6 (top), 10 (all), 11 (all), 12 (all), 13 (all), 14 (all), 15 (all), 16, 17 (all), 18 (all), 19, 20, 21, 22, 23 (all), 24 (all), 25, 26 (all), 27 (all), 28 (all), 29, 30 (all), 31 (all), 32 (all), 33, 34, 35 (all), 37 (right), 38, 39 (all), 40 (all), 41, 42 (left), 42-43 (background), 43 (all), 44 (all), 44-45 (background), 46 (all), 46-47 (background), 48 (all), 48-49 (background), 50-51 (background), 53, 54, 55, 56, 58 (all), 59, 60, 61 (all); Wikimedia Commons, p. 8; Wright brothers/Wikimedia Commons, p. 7

Design Elements: Adobe Stock (paper, Polaroid frame, sticky notes, tacks); Shutterstock Images (car leather texture, engine texture, fiber texture)

Library of Congress Control Number: 2024938323

PUBLISHER'S CATALOGING-IN-PUBLICATION DATA

Names: Kuehl, Ashley, author.
Title: Become a vehicle mechanic: car maintenance, bike repair & more / by Ashley Kuehl
Other Title: car maintenance, bike repair & more
Description: Minneapolis, Minnesota : ABDO Publishing, 2025 | Series: Talent to trade | Includes online resources and index.
Identifiers: ISBN 9781098294991 (lib. bdg.) | ISBN 9798384915041 (ebook)
Subjects: LCSH: Mechanics (Persons)--Juvenile literature. | Machinery--Maintenance and repair--Juvenile literature. | Bicycles--Maintenance and repair--Juvenile literature. | Repairing trades--Juvenile literature. | Jobs--Juvenile literature. | Trades--Juvenile literature.
Classification: DDC 629.287--dc23

CONTENTS

Talent to Trade 5

The Basics 7

Career Paths 21

    Automotive & Diesel
    Mechanic/Technician 21

    Automotive Body
    & Glass Repairer 26

    Motorcycle
    Mechanic/Technician 30

    Bicycle Mechanic 34

    Marine Vehicle Technician 38

Do It Yourself 42

Skills in Real Life 52

Glossary 62

Online Resources 63

Index 64

TALENT TO TRADE

Do you love figuring out how engines work? Are you tempted to fix broken vehicle systems? Do you feel comfortable using tools? If you answered yes to any of these questions, you might enjoy a career as a vehicle mechanic. This is someone who fixes and maintains automobiles, motorcycles, boats, and more.

Becoming a vehicle mechanic requires a lot of determination and hard work. Mechanics need to be comfortable spending their time in repair shops, maintaining and fixing vehicles. But if you love the challenge and you don't mind a little engine grease, the hard work will be worth it.

In this book, you'll learn a little about the history of vehicles and vehicle repair. You'll also learn about various jobs in the industry. You will explore the tools, skills, and techniques that vehicle mechanics use every day. You'll find inspiration and sources for education and training to build your own career. And you'll learn ways to turn your talents into a trade.

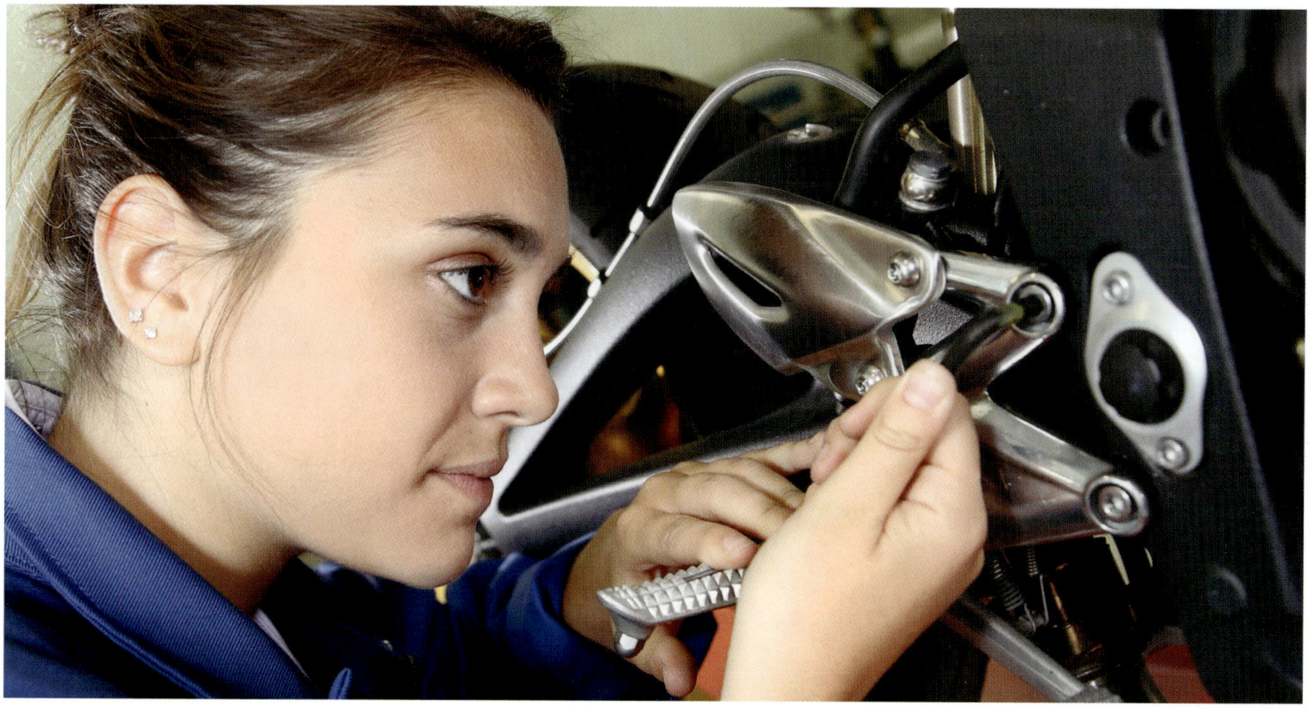

Around the eighth century, Vikings started to make longboats. These were some of the first European boats able to travel on the ocean.

Von Drais's bicycle had two wheels, a seat, and a steering mechanism. Riders used their feet to push it forward.

THE BASICS

HISTORY OF VEHICLES & VEHICLE REPAIR

Humans have been building and fixing vehicles for thousands of years. Ancient Egyptians built the first sailing boats around 4000 BCE. And with the invention of the wheel came the development of carts and wagons. These ancient vehicles relied on wind, animals, and manpower to move. If owners couldn't easily fix their vehicles, they usually took them to woodworkers or blacksmiths for repairs.

In 1698, Thomas Savery invented the steam engine. And by the 1800s, steamships were crossing oceans. Then in 1817, Karl von Drais invented a two-wheeled vehicle in Germany. Many historians consider it to be the first bicycle. In the 1860s, multiple inventors developed pedal bicycles. This included the penny-farthing, a tall bicycle with a big front wheel and a small back wheel.

British engineer Harry Lawson invented the safety bicycle around 1871. It had two wheels at the same height, a chain, and a sprocket. Riders' feet could also touch the ground, making it safer than other, taller bicycles. In the late 1860s, Sylvester H. Roper invented a steam-powered bicycle in Boston,

The Wright Brothers, famous for building early airplanes, first started a bicycle shop. They built and sold their own custom bikes.

Massachusetts. Many historians consider it to be the first American motorcycle.

In the 1890s, safety bicycles were imported to the United States. Companies started to mass-produce bicycles and people opened bike shops. These shops sold bicycles and accessories and offered repair services.

In 1853, the invention of the internal combustion engine led to the development of gas-powered vehicles. In 1886, Karl Benz introduced the first gas-powered automobile in Germany. The Benz Patent-Motorwagen had three wheels and a bench seat big enough for two people.

Automobile manufacturers soon needed a way to safely deliver their products to customers. In 1898, automobile company owner Alexander Winton built the first semitruck and trailer in Cleveland, Ohio. As more roads were developed, people used diesel-powered trucks to haul goods across long distances. Over time, these trucks were improved to be easier to use and more productive, becoming the modern semitruck used by truckers today.

Before the 1900s, vehicle manufacturers made automobiles in small quantities. Many were custom-built and expensive to produce and buy. So, they were

In 1888, Bertha Benz drove a Model 3 Benz Patent-Motorwagen over 62 miles (100 km) to visit her mother. This was the first long distance journey taken by an automobile.

Ford sold more than 15 million Model T automobiles between 1908 and 1927.

mostly owned by the wealthy. Though some manufacturers provided repair services, maintenance was mostly left up to the vehicle's owner. Automobile owners hired drivers, who were also knowledgeable on maintenance and repairs.

This all changed in 1908 when Henry Ford introduced and started mass-producing the Model T, the first affordable automobile in the world. Other companies began mass-producing automobiles over the next decades. As more automobiles were made, both manufacturers and private businesses began to offer maintenance and repair services.

In the 2020s, vehicle designers and engineers are working to improve electric and solar-powered engines. And the automobile service industry is expected to grow about 2 percent between 2022 and 2032. In the following pages, you'll learn what it takes to work in the vehicle service and repair industry. You may even be inspired to start your own journey toward a career in vehicle mechanics.

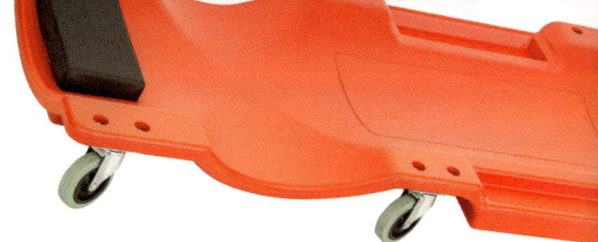

TOOLS OF THE TRADE

Explore some of the tools that vehicle mechanics and technicians use to inspect and repair automobiles, diesel vehicles, motorcycles, bicycles, and boats.

AUTO & DIESEL MECHANIC/ TECHNICIAN

ENGINE DIAGNOSTIC SOFTWARE TOOL

All modern automobiles and diesel vehicles come with a computer called the electronic control unit (ECU). It gathers and records data from different sensors inside the vehicle. A diagnostic software tool can be plugged into the ECU and it reads what was recorded. If it finds a problem, it provides an error code. The mechanic uses that code to help find the problem before looking inside the vehicle.

VEHICLE LIFT

Most of the working parts of an automobile or diesel vehicle are located under its hood or body. To access the vehicle's underside, mechanics may use a machine called a vehicle lift. There are different types of lifts, but all have large metal beams that hold the vehicle. These beams are usually attached to posts or a system connected to the floor of the auto or repair shop. Mechanics can raise the beams to the height they need before locking them in place.

CREEPER

A creeper is a mostly flat piece of hard material attached to four or more wheels. The mechanic lies down on it, face up, and rolls under a vehicle. Then they can reach up to work on the underside of the vehicle. Using a creeper means mechanics don't have to bend their necks or backs at uncomfortable angles.

WORK LIGHTS

To see into dark spaces within a vehicle, mechanics may use different types of lights. A floor lamp has a larger frame, often on wheels, with one or more light panels attached. Under-hood lights tend to be long and thin, with hooks or magnets that attach to the vehicle. A headlamp is a battery-powered light attached to a headband, which leaves a mechanic's hands free to work.

DRAIN PANS, DRIP PANS & FUNNELS

Before draining any vehicle fluids, a mechanic first places a drain pan under the vehicle. Drain pans are plastic or metal containers that catch and store vehicle fluids. A mechanic may also place a drip pan under the drain pan. Drip pans are large plastic or metal trays that catch excess fluids. When adding new fluids to the vehicle, the tech may also use a funnel to avoid spills.

WRENCHES

Mechanics use different wrenches to tighten and loosen different nuts and bolts. For example, they use a cross-armed or four-way lug wrench on lug nuts which hold tires and hubcaps in place. Lug wrenches have two metal rods stuck together in an X shape. Gas powered vehicles have spark plugs. Removing or replacing them requires a spark plug wrench. This tool has one long, thin metal cylinder attached to a shorter, thicker one.

CRIMPING TOOLS

Crimping is one way to install or replace cables or wires. A crimping connecter is a small piece of metal with holes for the cable or wire to go through. A crimp tool is similar to pliers. It pinches the crimp connector tightly around the cables or wires, forming a seal.

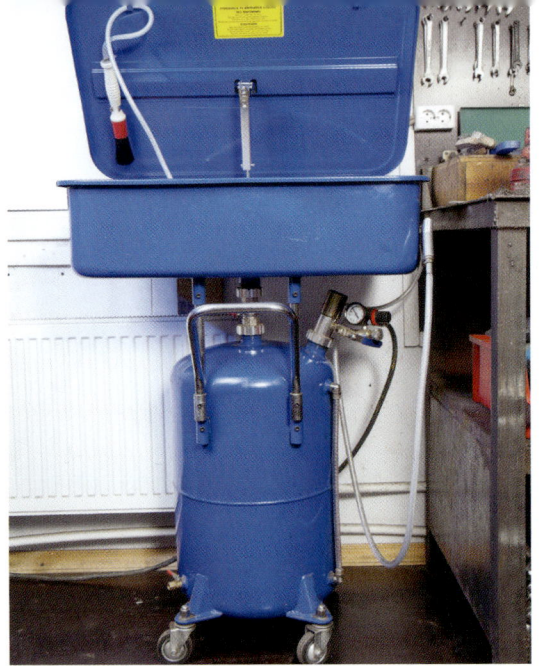

PARTS WASHER

Engine parts get dirty with use, causing problems with functionality. Mechanics may clean parts, such as valves, pistons, and transmissions. This can help the parts work better or make it easier to find cracks. One type of parts washer is similar to a big dishwasher. Mechanics put dirty parts on a tray, add a cleaning solution, and then use a high-pressure sprayer to clean the parts.

AUTOMOTIVE BODY & GLASS REPAIRER

PNEUMATIC DENT PULLER

A pneumatic dent puller is a long tool with a handle on one end and a suction cup on the other end. The suction cup is attached in or over a dent in the vehicle's body. Then the repairer pulls the handle to flatten the dent or move the piece of metal into a new shape.

GLUE TAB

A glue tab is a flat tool with a hook or knob on one side. It comes in different shapes and sizes. The tab is attached to the dent with hot glue. Once it cools and sticks, the repairer pulls the hook or knob, flattening the dent. Then they spray the glue with alcohol to loosen it and easily remove the tab.

KNOCKDOWNS

Knockdowns are cylinder-shaped tools. Repairers hit one end with a special hammer to remove dents. These tools have different shaped tips for different types of dents. For example, a round steel knockdown

can easily flatten a large dent. And a thin tip knockdown can flatten a small, sharp dent.

EDGE PLIERS

Repairers use edge pliers to flatten dented or bent edges of a metal panel. This can be the edge of the vehicle's door. Edge pliers usually have one or two flat pads on one side and a removable tip on the other side. Most come with many different shaped tips for different types of dents. The tool attaches around the panel's edge. The repairer squeezes the pliers and rocks it back and forth, flattening the dent or bent edge with the tip.

BUFFER & POLISHER

An electric buffer or polisher smooths out the surface of the vehicle once repairs are complete. This device has a soft pad on a flat rotating disk. A liquid polish is used on the pad, which then spins over the surface.

MOTORCYCLE TECHNICIAN

DYNAMOMETER

A dynamometer, or dyno, looks like a treadmill for vehicles. It attaches to a computer system with gauges that gathers data from the vehicle's systems. This includes horsepower, force, fuel usage, and more.

SCREWDRIVERS & WRENCHES

To access the engine and other parts of a motorcycle, techs remove the seat, side panels, and other protective coverings. They do this by using screwdrivers and wrenches. Socket wrenches are used to loosen and tighten spark plugs.

BEAD BREAKER & TIRE IRON

Bead breaker tools come in many different shapes and sizes. But all of them work by applying force to separate the tire from the wheel rim. Tire irons are long metal tools with a flat hooked end that is used to push the tire out of the rim.

MULTIMETER

A multimeter is a handheld electronic device with cables. The cables are attached to the battery when the motorcycle is not running. When the tech starts the motorcycle, the multimeter measures the battery's voltage.

BICYCLE MECHANIC

REPAIR STAND

Bike mechanics usually use a repair stand to fix bicycles. This aluminum stand has a long post with a short arm and clamp at the top. The clamp holds the bicycle frame above the ground and keeps it still.

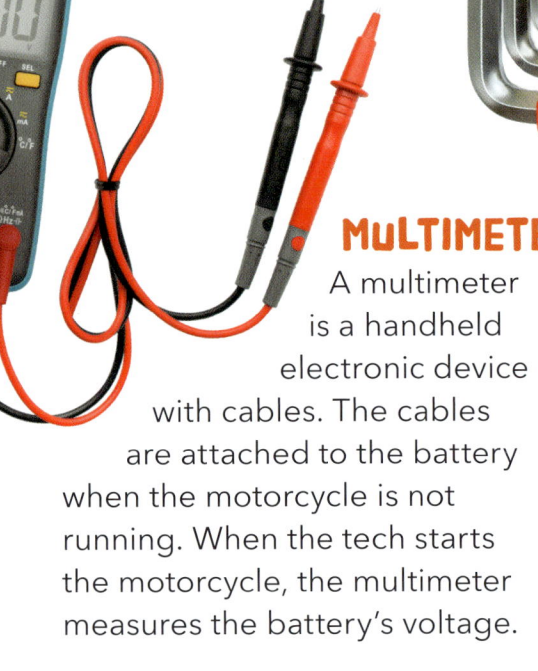

HEX WRENCHES

Hex wrenches are six-sided metal tools. Mechanics use these tools to loosen or tighten hexagon-shaped sockets, common on bicycles. Hex wrenches usually come in a set with multiple sizes.

CHAIN WHIP & LOCKRING

A bike's cassette is a group of metal wheels with teeth that the chain goes around. To safely remove the bike chain from the cassette, mechanics may use a chain whip and a lockring. A chain whip is a bar with a short bike chain attached. A lockring is a special type of wrench. The mechanic hooks the chain whip's chain onto the teeth of the cassette to hold it in place. Then they use the lockring to loosen or tighten the bolt that holds the cassette in place.

CHAIN TOOL

Bike chains are made of steel plates that are held together by rivets. When the chain links break, mechanics may use a chain tool. This is a metal piece with a gap and driving pin. The mechanic places the chain into the gap and turns the driving pin to push rivets in or out of the chain.

TIRE PUMP

A bike tire pump is a metal cylinder on a small floor stand. It has an attached tube and removable pump head that connects to the air valve.

Different bikes have different valves, so mechanics usually have multiple pump heads. Almost all pumps have an attached air pressure gauge. The mechanic uses the gauge to see how much air is in the tire.

MARINE VEHICLE TECHNICIAN

WIRE BRUSH & CORROSION INHIBITOR

A common problem with watercraft is built-up dirt or oil on parts of the engine or other systems. Techs rub a wire brush over the dirt to clean it off. To prevent corrosion, techs will use an anti-corrosion spray with the wire brush.

HOSE REMOVAL PICK & HOSE CLAMP PLIERS

Sometimes tubes and hoses on watercraft wear out and need to be replaced. To remove them, techs may use a hose removal pick. This is a long tool with a small hook on one end that can pull tubes out. Sometimes a tube clamp, a small, hard circular piece, holds the tube in place. Hose clamp pliers can reach into small areas to tightly pinch and open the clamp.

OIL CHANGE PUMP

To change the oil in a boat, techs usually suction it out with an oil change pump. The pump has a tube that attaches to the watercraft's oil reservoir. The pump's crank starts the flow of oil through the tube into its reservoir.

SOLDERING IRON

A soldering iron is a handheld tool with a small metal tube that shoots out a small, precise flame. A tech may use this to heat-shrink a wire connection. It can also smooth frayed rope edges.

SAFETY GEAR

Marine technicians need to protect themselves when working on boats. They usually wear non-slip shoes that have steel toes. These protect them from slipping on wet surfaces or from falling tools or equipment. Safety glasses protect the tech's eyes from water and engine fluids. And a headlamp can help them see into small, dark parts of the watercraft.

SPECIAL SKILLS

Explore some of the skills that vehicle mechanics need to do their jobs.

ATTENTION TO DETAIL

Most vehicle mechanics and techs offer standard maintenance services in addition to repairs. The right levels of fluids and adjustments can make big differences in how well a vehicle works and how long its parts last. A good mechanic and tech can spot small details when making sure parts and systems are functioning.

COMMUNICATION

Mechanics and techs mostly work on vehicles that belong to other people. The mechanic or tech needs to listen to any issues a customer has, including details of which parts aren't working or need attention. Once an issue is found, they need to clearly explain the problem, how they will fix it, and how much the work will cost.

DEXTERITY

Mechanics and techs use a variety of hand tools and heavy machinery. Vehicles are made of many different parts and systems. So, workers need to be able to adjust small parts, work in cramped spaces, empty and fill fluids without spills, and more. These tasks all require good hand-eye coordination.

ENGINES & ELECTRICAL SYSTEMS KNOWLEDGE

Manufactures make different kinds of vehicles with different types of engines and electrical systems. Mechanics and techs need to have strong knowledge of how those engines and systems work and fit together. This can include understanding the roles and responsibilities of each component. It also includes understanding how each part affects the others.

MULTITASKING & PRIORITIZING

On any given day, mechanics and techs are likely working on several vehicles. These may all need maintenance or repairs on multiple parts and systems. Sometimes new parts need to be ordered. And customers want to know when they'll get their vehicles back. Good mechanics and techs can estimate how long maintenance or repairs may take. They also know how to multitask and prioritize tasks to work efficiently.

PROBLEM-SOLVING & PERSISTENCE

A customer may not know why their vehicle isn't working, just that something's wrong. And a warning light or funny noise could be caused by a variety of problems. Mechanics and techs need to be persistent when testing and checking parts and systems to figure out what's causing the issue. And they may need to try different solutions to fix the problem.

CAREER PATHS

CAREERS IN VEHICLE REPAIR AND MAINTENANCE

There are many different types of vehicle mechanics and technicians. Many focus their skills and expertise on specific vehicles or specialties. Let's investigate some career paths for those interested in working on vehicles.

AUTOMOTIVE & DIESEL MECHANIC/ TECHNICIAN

Automotive mechanics or techs and diesel mechanics or techs both have very similar skills and duties. The biggest difference between them are the types of vehicles they work on. An auto mechanic or tech works on automobiles with gas or hybrid engines. They often work at auto repair shops or at a dealership's service center. A diesel mechanic or tech works on vehicles with diesel engines. In the United States, most diesel engines are on bigger vehicles, like semitrucks or buses. Bulldozers, tractors, cranes, and some automobiles have diesel engines too. Diesel techs usually work in repair shops or may travel to a worksite to repair vehicles.

The words *mechanic* and *technician* are sometimes used interchangeably for these jobs. The main difference is that a mechanic tends to do more hands-on work. And a tech may have more experience using computer diagnostics for troubleshooting.

MAINTENANCE CHECK

During a maintenance check, mechanics inspect all vehicle fluids, parts, and systems. Fluids help automobiles or diesel vehicles run safely and efficiently. These include brake fluid, transmission fluid, power steering fluid, coolant, and more. Most fluids are stored in reservoirs that can be accessed under the hood. Mechanics check these and may refill or replace fluids if needed.

Mechanics also check other parts such as the wheels, tires, belts, hoses, brakes, and more. They may make small fixes such as adding air to tires. If they find problems that require more extensive repairs such as replacing any parts, they will alert the customer, who can then decide how they want to proceed.

OIL CHANGE

Motor oil is a thick liquid that helps parts of the engine move smoothly and keeps them from overheating. Over time, the oil collects dirt and bits of air, reducing its ability to work properly. To change the oil, a mechanic removes the oil dipstick and drain plug to drain the oil into a pan below the vehicle. The mechanic then inspects the oil chamber before replacing the plug and installing a new oil filter. They add new oil and run the engine, making sure nothing leaks.

TIRE ROTATION

Automobiles and diesel vehicles may drive many miles, which causes tire wear. Each tire wears a little differently depending on its location on the vehicle. To keep tire wear as consistent as possible, vehicles need to periodically have their tires rotated. The mechanic removes each tire and moves it to a different spot. They may also flip the tires around, so the side that was near the middle of the vehicle is moved to the outside. This way, the tires end up with similar wear and tear, making them last longer.

DIAGNOSTIC TESTS

Customers often bring their vehicles to mechanics or techs because of a problem. For example, the brakes don't work, a warning light turned on, or their vehicle is making a strange sound. The mechanic listens to the customer's concerns before running tests on the vehicle.

Mechanics follow a checklist when inspecting vehicle fluids, parts, and systems.

Oil changes are one of the most common maintenance services provided by auto and diesel repair shops.

Some shops specialize in tires. They may offer deals where a customer can get free tire rotations if they purchase tires from the shop.

When reviewing an estimate with a customer, mechanics need to be able to answer questions and address customer concerns.

Depending on the issue, mechanics may use a diagnostic software tool to help narrow down what's wrong.

PLAN & ESTIMATE

After finding the problem, mechanics decide on how they think it should be repaired. This could be replacing a brake pad or transmission. But before they do any work, the mechanic writes up a detailed estimate. This includes how long repairs may take, what parts they may need, and the estimated cost. Then they review that estimate with the customer to see if they want to move forward with the repair.

REPAIR & REPLACE

Once a customer approves the repair, the mechanic gets to work. Repair work might mean replacing parts such as drive belts, brake pads or rotors, or the battery. If the vehicle isn't moving properly, the mechanic will usually check the suspension system. The suspension keeps vehicles from veering off to one side or bouncing up and down too much. It also keeps all the wheels on the ground. Mechanics might replace or realign suspension parts called struts. Suspension problems can also move wheels. After fixing any

suspension issues, the mechanic will realign the wheels, making sure that they line up correctly.

TRACKING WORK

As they inspect and repair, the mechanic takes notes on what they do, any parts replaced, and the service date. They also note the condition of the engine and system parts. This information is entered into the company's database, which keeps records of vehicles and work completed. That helps customers know when to come back for another inspection and how long vehicle components might last.

Mechanics may also know what work needs to be done based on how many miles a vehicle has driven. Many automobile manufacturers recommend certain types of maintenance to be done when a vehicle hits a milestone. One milestone could be 100,000 miles driven since the automobile was manufactured.

AUTOMOTIVE BODY & GLASS REPAIRER

Some vehicle technicians specialize in fixing automobiles after accidents or other exterior damage. They focus on parts such as the windows and the body, or frame, of the vehicle, rather than what makes it run.

DAMAGE EVALUATION

When a damaged vehicle arrives, the repairer looks closely at all parts of its body, including windows. They figure out which parts they can repair and what needs to be replaced. Next, they plan how to get the vehicle back to how it was before the damage. Then they put together a detailed estimate including parts, labor, and total cost. The repairer shares this with the vehicle's owner or insurance company before moving forward with the repair.

DENT REMOVAL

A big part of a repairer's job is fixing and straightening bent or dented metal pieces of a vehicle's body. Sometimes repair workers remove parts such as vehicle doors to reach underneath a dented panel. Workers use different techniques and tools depending on the dent. They might push or hit the frame from the inside to force it back into place or pull the dent from the outside.

Many repair shops work directly with insurance companies when submitting cost estimates and invoices.

A repairer often uses different techniques and multiple tools to fix one dent.

Repairers wear special safety helmets when welding. These protect them against burns from sparks. Most helmets also come with auto-darkening lenses to prevent damage to the worker's eyes.

Repairers wear masks when sanding or painting. This protects them from breathing in small particles or chemicals.

WELDING

Workers may weld parts together or weld cracks in the vehicle's body. This might include welding a vehicle frame that has been damaged. Or they may weld cracked wheels that have been damaged by potholes. After putting on safety gear, they apply a very thin flame to the metal. Welding can also help fix rust spots or warped metal parts. The repairer cuts off the rusty or warped piece of metal before welding a new metal patch in place.

SANDING, PAINTING & FINISHING

A repairer usually sands down the surface of the new or repaired pieces of metal to smooth out any rough spots. Once repairs are complete, workers repaint the parts of the vehicle they worked on. First, they find the right paint color by mixing and matching the new paint to the vehicle's paint. Then, they usually spray a layer of primer on the metal, followed by several coats of paint. Finally, repairers buff and polish out any remaining scratches and bumps on the paint's surface.

MOTORCYCLE MECHANIC/ TECHNICIAN

A motorcycle mechanic or technician repairs and maintains motorcycles and other motorized vehicles with two wheels.

TUNE-UPS

A tune-up for a motorcycle is a routine maintenance check. Techs often use a diagnostic software tool to check the motorcycle's systems so they know what needs to be adjusted. Tune-ups can include replacing brake pads and fluids and changing or cleaning air filters. Techs also inspect and replace spark plugs if needed.

Some customers may want a dyno-tune. This ensures their motorcycles are getting the best horsepower, torque, and fuel usage. During this service, techs will run the motorcycle on a dyno. The test's data helps the tech know which parts and systems they need to adjust such as the ignition, fuel, and air supply.

TIRE CHECKS & REPLACEMENT

Techs also check the motorcycle's tires for wear, damage, and pressure. First, they look for holes and examine the tire tread. Legally, the tread must be 0.03 inches (0.8 mm) thick. If it's thinner, the tire must be replaced. Mechanics also check tire pressure. If tire pressure is low, it can mean the tire needs air, or it has a leak and needs to be patched or replaced.

To replace a tire, techs first break the bead, or seal between the tire and wheel rim. This seal keeps air from leaking out of the tire. Techs insert a bead breaker into the seal to create a gap. Then they use a tire iron as a lever to push the edge of the tire out of the wheel rim.

Tune-ups are important to ensure motorcycles work safely.

Some shops will have specialized machines to help them change tires more efficiently.

Some auto parts stores will test batteries for free.

Some shops specialize in building or modifying custom motorcycles.

BATTERY TESTING

A motorcycle's battery powers the headlights, starter, and dashboard electronics. During a maintenance check, a tech inspects the battery and its connections to look for leaks or corrosion. They may also use a multimeter to check the electrical flow. This provides information on the battery's condition. If needed, they may replace the battery before testing the electronics and starting the engine.

UPGRADES & MODIFICATIONS

Some motorcycle owners want to personalize their bikes. For example, they may want to add turbochargers to make their motorcycles go faster. Experienced techs know which size turbocharger works with which engines. Techs may adjust the fuel intake system too. Other owners may want to make their motorcycles more comfortable or change the look. A tech can do this by replacing or adjusting the suspension, the handlebars, or the steering system.

BICYCLE MECHANIC

A bicycle mechanic usually works in a bike repair shop, which is often part of a retail store. They maintain and fix bikes, as well as providing customer support.

TUNE-UPS

During most basic tune-ups, bike mechanics clean, lubricate, and inspect all of the bike's components including the tires, brakes, gears, chain, cassette, frame, handlebars, seat, and pedals. Mechanics may also look and listen for any strange sounds or loose pieces. Then they will make any minor adjustments and complete a safety check to make sure all parts are properly working. They may also suggest major repairs or further maintenance if needed.

REPAIRS & ASSEMBLY

Mechanics also make significant repairs or replace any components that aren't working properly. These can include the brake pads, wheel spokes, gear-shifting cables, suspension systems, and more. Mechanics also build custom bikes. Once the major repair or assembly job is completed, mechanics make sure all parts are working properly and test ride the bike.

Shops usually offer multiple tune-up services. The more expensive tune-ups include better services, such as a more thorough inspection, and may include more major repairs.

When building a bike, mechanics need to consider what the customer wants as well as their budget.

Bike shop employees need to be knowledgeable about the products they sell. This way, they can help customers decide what products best fit their needs.

TIRES

All bikes have tires and inner tubes. Tires give a bike traction and speed and protect the inner tube. The inner tube is placed between the tire and wheel frame. It inflates and provides the bike with suspension and support. Mechanics typically only replace the inner tube when fixing a flat tire. But if the tire is worn out or cracked, the inner tube will also need to be replaced. The last step is to inflate the tire and check again for leaks.

SCHEDULING & INVENTORY

Sometimes multiple customers bring bicycles in for repair at the same time. Mechanics need to be able to estimate how long repairs will take and work efficiently to ensure bikes are finished within the time frame they give the customer. To make repairs, the shop also needs to have replacement parts in stock. Taking inventory means knowing how much of everything is in the shop. That helps a mechanic or shop manager decide what they need to order from suppliers.

MARINE VEHICLE TECHNICIAN

A marine vehicle technician works on boats, ships, and other water vehicles. They may work for boat manufacturers or dealerships, on individual ships or boats, or at marinas.

OIL CHANGES

There's not much space under a boat, so techs may pump oil out with an extraction pump. When the oil chamber is empty, the tech changes the oil filter. Then they refill the system with new oil.

ENGINE MAINTENANCE

Watercraft engines get dirty, especially when moving through dirty water. Cleaning the engine is part of a regular maintenance service. The tech waits until the engine is cool and then detaches the battery connections. They brush any dirt off all engine parts and spray it with compressed air. Then they use a degreaser and cloth to wipe off any oil buildup before rinsing the engine with clean water. Having a clean engine helps techs troubleshoot problems, as it makes broken or loose parts easier to see.

Boat manuals usually include a service schedule for what maintenance needs to be done and when.

Many technicians offer mobile services. They will travel to their customer to complete maintenance so the owner doesn't have to move their boat.

Professional techs will also inspect the boat's systems and parts. They will alert the owner if any additional services need to be done.

If there's a lot of damage, a tech may replace the entire propeller.

FUEL & ELECTRICAL SYSTEMS

Techs need to figure out what's wrong when a boat is making weird noises or smells funny. The tech may start by checking fuel systems for leaks or cracks. They also examine the electrical system and battery voltage. A low battery may need to be replaced. And dirt or oil buildup and corrosion can cause electrical issues. After their inspections, techs clean and repair or replace any parts as needed.

PROPELLER REPAIR

The propeller has blades that spin like a fan and is usually located on the back of a watercraft. It's connected to the engine and pushes the boat forward. If a propeller blade is bent, the tech may hammer it flat again. If it has a crack or hole, techs may attach a new piece or patch. Finally, they use an electric grinder to soften any rough sides or edges before sanding or buffing the metal to smooth it out.

⌐ DO IT YOURSELF ¬

IGNITE YOUR
VISION

It's time to get creative! What are your favorite types of vehicles? If you could design any vehicle, what would it look like? Create a vision board that reflects this and inspires you. Let it motivate you to turn your talents into your trade!

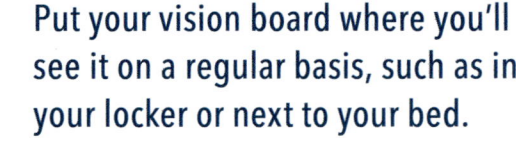

Put your vision board where you'll see it on a regular basis, such as in your locker or next to your bed.

Imagine and design your ideal vehicle.

TUNE UP YOUR KNOWLEDGE

You've got the passion, vision, and motivation. Even if you aren't ready to start formal training, you can still take steps to develop and grow your knowledge of vehicles and vehicle repair.

Visit a vehicle museum. Many museums do their own restoration, maintenance, and engine work and are usually happy to share their knowledge.

Find a vehicle club or meet-up near you. Enthusiasts love to talk about their favorite vehicles and engines. They may also provide education around vehicle maintenance.

Watch vehicle repair and maintenance videos to learn different methods and techniques.

ACCELERATE YOUR EXPERIENCE

You don't have to wait until you're an adult to practice your skills! Start by working on small projects to develop the skill sets needed for mechanical work.

Build a model car to help you learn more about a full-size version.

Offer to help an adult who does their own bicycle repairs or vehicle maintenance. You'll get to see the process up close and maybe test out some tools.

Enroll in an industrial arts, mechanics, or metal shop class to learn basic mechanical and repair skills.

WORK ON YOUR SKILLS

Find the people in your life who can help you grow your talents. And find ways to help those around you! You'll develop your people skills as well as your mechanical skills.

Volunteer to wash or clean out your family's or a friend's vehicle. It'll give you a closer look at some of the parts mechanics and body repairers know so well.

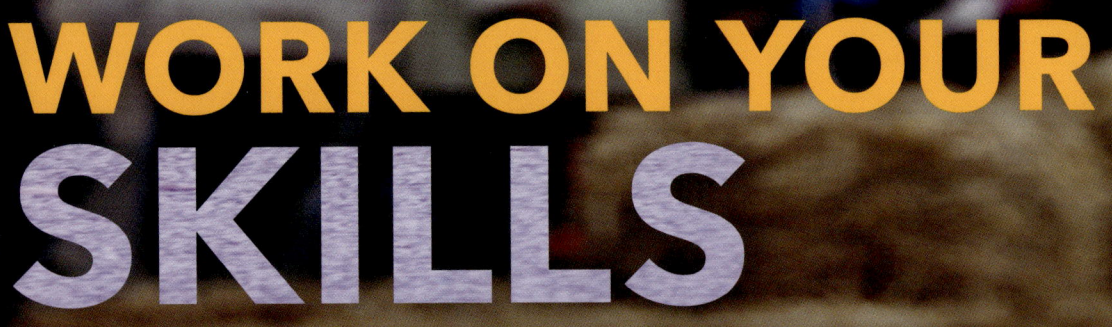

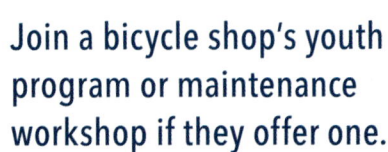

Join a bicycle shop's youth program or maintenance workshop if they offer one.

FIX YOUR OWN FLAT BIKE TIRE

An easy way to start working on vehicles is to change the tire on your bike!

Tip! Always inspect your tire before inserting a new inner tube. If there are any existing sharp objects, they can damage your new inner tube.

step 4

SUPPLIES

bike
2 tire levers
patch kit (optional)
new bike tire (optional)
new inner tube
bike pump

Step 10

STEPS

1. Follow your bike's manual or the manufacturer's website to remove the wheel from your bike. Or ask an adult for help.

2. Deflate the inner tube by loosening the air valve cap. Set the cap aside.

3. At the opposite end of the wheel from the valve, hook the curved end of the tire lever under the tire bead. The tire lever's handle should be pointing away from the center of the wheel.

4. About a hand width away from the first tire lever, hook a second tire lever under the tire bead.

5. Push down on one tire lever to turn the handle towards the center of the wheel. Repeat this with the second lever. This will make the tire bead pop over the edge of the wheel rim.

6. Pull the tire to separate it from the wheel rim. Stop when you get to the valve. If there is a lockring on the valve, unscrew it first. Pull the valve through the wheel rim valve hole. Set the wheel rim aside.

7. Pull the valve to separate the inner tube from the tire. Recycle or throw away the old inner tube.

8. Check the tire for holes. If there are any sharp objects stuck in the tire, remove them and then patch the tire. If there is too much damage, you may need to replace the tire.

9. On the new inner tube, remove the dust cap and lock ring. Unfold the inner tube carefully. Connect the bike pump to the valve to partially inflate the inner tube so it holds its shape. Remove the pump and set it aside.

10. Position the tire and inner tube loosely around the wheel rim. Insert the valve into the wheel rim valve hole. Tuck the rest of the inner tube into the tire.

11. Using your hands, tuck the tire bead underneath the wheel rim. Start at the opposite end of the wheel from the valve. Tuck the tire into the wheel rim in both directions all the way around. Once you reach the valve end, hook the curved end of the tire lever into the tire bead so the handle is pointing towards the wheel center. Repeat with the second lever. Then push down to turn the handle away from the wheel center to pop the tire into place.

12. Finish inflating the inner tube and screw the air valve cap back on.

13. Follow your bike's manual or the manufacturer's website to attach the wheel back onto the bike. Or ask an adult for help.

SKILLS IN REAL LIFE

BECOMING A VEHICLE MECHANIC OR TECHNICIAN

EDUCATION

Most vehicle mechanics and techs who work with engines usually need to become certified first. Most trade and vocational schools offer the training needed for these certificates. These programs provide background knowledge of engine parts and systems, diagnosing problems, maintenance, and repair. Some also offer specialized courses on specific vehicle types.

The National Institute for Automotive Service Excellence offers a series of certificates for auto and diesel mechanics. These are the standard certificates for vehicle mechanics in the United States. Automobile techs may also get an associate's degree in math, electronics, or automotive repair. And some manufacturers and dealerships sponsor students working on their associate's degrees. These students take classes while working as an apprentice to a more experienced mechanic or tech.

The Motorcycle Mechanics Institute offers a certification for motorcycle techs. Techs may also decide to get an associate's degree in motorcycle or engine repair. And marine vehicle mechanics may get an associate's degree or certificate in marine engine technology or marine maintenance technology.

Some vehicle mechanics and techs who work with engines aren't required to have prior schooling or certificates. But most employers prefer their employees to have some background knowledge. Many mechanics and techs without prior schooling may start out as trainees or helpers.

You don't need a specialized degree to become a bicycle mechanic. Many bike shop managers hire and train new employees. But for those that want to have knowledge and skills before starting work, some high schools and colleges offer mechanic training programs. Students learn about bicycle tools, mechanics, materials, parts, customer service, and brake systems.

FINDING A JOB

Once you've met the requirements to work in your state, it's time to find a job!

JOB SEARCH TIPS

> Put together a résumé that describes your education and experience. Even if you haven't worked in the industry, include any activities or volunteer work that are relevant to the role, such as volunteering at the local bike shop or marina. Listing other previous jobs shows you are reliable and willing to learn.

> Keep in contact with teachers and classmates from your school. Ask them to connect you with people they know in the industry. This helps you grow your professional network and learn about job or training opportunities.

> Identify repair shops or marinas where you might like to work. Introduce yourself to the manager and ask for an informational interview to learn more about their business. Express your interest in working there, and give them a copy of your résumé.

> If you are invited to interview for a job, be prepared. Before the interview, research the business's history, mission statements, and offerings. Be ready to articulate why you want to work for the business and how you think you'd be a good fit for the role. Finally, have your own questions prepared for the interviewer. This shows you are thoughtful and serious about the job!

> Is there somewhere you really want to work, but there aren't any job openings for the role you're after? Consider applying for a different role, such as an assistant, a cleaner, or a receptionist. This tactic puts you in a strong position to be considered for your desired position when it is available.

KEEP GOING

The learning doesn't stop once you land a job. Many mechanics and techs must renew their certificates every few years. Even if additional training isn't required, it's important to seek out opportunities for professional development.

Over time, safety rules can change. So do materials and best practices for your work. And since engineers and manufacturers continue to change and improve their vehicles, you'll need to stay up to date on new types of engines and systems. You might also further your education with additional courses or specialized training. These can help you get higher-level jobs or focus more closely on particular areas.

Additional training can also help you learn new methods and how to work more efficiently.

MEET A PRO: JOHN MAXWELL, PRO MOTORCYCLE MECHANIC

When John Maxwell was 13, he bought a motorcycle magazine before a long flight and fell in love with motorcycles. For an eighth-grade research project, he studied motorcycle manufacturer Harley-Davidson. He bought his first motorcycle at age 23, and a few years later, he learned about a trade school where he could learn motorcycle mechanics.

While Maxwell studied, he worked at a Harley-Davidson retail store. And after he graduated, he worked as a mechanic for the company. He even started his own YouTube channel, where he shares information and answers questions about Harley-Davidson motorcycles. In 2020, Maxwell opened his own motorcycle shop specializing in American motorcycles.

TRADES AT WORK

EARNING POTENTIAL

The US Bureau of Labor Statistics provides estimated wage ranges for most workers in any given job category. The ranges below are from May 2023. While these estimates provide a sense of what you could expect to earn, actual salaries can vary greatly depending on where you work, your level of experience, and any specialized skills you have.

GROW YOUR POTENTIAL

Whatever salary you start at, you can grow your earning potential throughout your career. Here are a few ways you can boost your income while continuing to do what you love.

Specialize in a specific vehicle type or service. A mechanic might specialize in engines, transmissions, or suspension systems. Or they might become an expert for a particular manufacturer. Some techs focus on specific electrical systems or paint and bodywork. A diesel mechanic or tech might focus on farm equipment, trains, or construction vehicles.

Become your own boss. When you're self-employed, your earnings can increase with your experience and the success of your business.

JOB CATEGORY	ANNUAL SALARY
Automotive Service Technicians and Mechanics	$37,000–$62,000
Diesel Engine Specialists	$48,000–$70,000
Auto Body and Related Repairers	$41,000–$62,000
Motorcycle Mechanics	$37,000–$58,000
Bicycle Repairers	$34,000–$45,000
Motorboat Mechanics and Service Technicians	$42,000–$61,000

FINANCIAL SMARTS

However you make money, it's important to manage your finances wisely.

If you have an employer, you will receive a regular paycheck from them. This income will be your wages minus taxes. If your employer offers health insurance, retirement savings, or any other benefits, those will also be deducted from your take-home pay. Financial experts recommend you put about 20 percent of each paycheck into savings and try to keep an emergency fund with enough money to cover three to six months' worth of living expenses.

For example, self-employment may mean managing or opening a repair shop. Or you might invest in your own equipment and travel to the vehicles that need repairs.

Break into a new area of the industry. Consider specific clients who want something unique. You might focus on restoring vintage cars or motorcycles. Or you might work to become mechanic for a race car team.

If you are self-employed, you will receive payments directly from your clients. You'll need to track this income along with your business expenses, such as tools. Self-employed individuals must also pay their own taxes, generally four times a year, since they don't have an employer withholding taxes from each paycheck. Business owners use the remaining profits to pay themselves as well as fund savings accounts—for both themselves and their business!

If you have employees, you must pay both your employees and yourself. You will manage your company's payroll, employee benefits, business insurance, and more. This takes a lot of work and organization! But hiring employees can let you take on bigger and more complex jobs. It can also give you more time to focus on growing the business.

DO WHAT YOU LOVE!

Working as a vehicle mechanic requires determination, an interest in how machines work, and attention to detail. Finding success in this field can take years of learning about engines and mechanical training. Many people in this industry find that the hard work is worth the reward of being able to fix a difficult engine problem or get a vehicle running again.

Perhaps you dream of working in a repair shop solving tricky mechanical problems. Or you want to work on a marina fixing boats. Maybe you see yourself rebuilding classic motorcycles or automobiles. Or your goal is to work for your favorite auto manufacturer or dealership. As long as you do what you love, you'll love what you do.

GLOSSARY

articulate—to clearly and effectively express oneself.

component—one of the parts or units of a combination, mixture, or system.

corrosion—when a material is worn away gradually, usually by a chemical substance.

diagnose—to recognize something, such as a disease, by signs, symptoms, or tests. Diagnostic methods are used to study something to find a problem.

diesel—a fuel designed for use in diesel engines.

drive belt—long rubber strips that move power through different parts of an engine and to other moving parts.

efficient—in a way that does not waste time or energy.

gauge—a measuring device.

hubcap—a metal cap on a vehicle's wheel that covers the end of the axle.

interchangeable—in place of each other.

periodic—repeating at regular intervals of time.

piston—a part in an engine that moves up and down inside the cylinder.

pneumatic—filled with air under pressure.

potential—capable of being or becoming.

primer—a material used to prepare a surface for paint.

prioritize—to list in order of importance.

reservoir—a place where something is stored.

rivet—a metal piece that holds things together.

software—the written programs used by a computer.

solder—to unite or repair using a melted mixture of metals.

spark plug—small devices in an engine that light the fuel.

specialize—to develop expertise in a certain area, called a specialty. Specialized means suited to a particular purpose or occupation.

sponsor—to provide financial support.

struts—parts located near a vehicle's wheels that help absorb bouncing movement, also known as shock absorbers.

technician—someone who is skilled at a task requiring special knowledge. A technique is a way of doing a task using special knowledge or skills.

torque—a force that causes turning or twisting.

troubleshoot—to find and fix issues.

turbocharger—a device that compresses gas and forces air into an internal combustion engine.

vocational—relating to training in a skill or trade to be pursued as a career.

voltage—electric force measured in volts.

wheel spoke—a bar that connects a wheel rim to the center wheel piece.

ONLINE RESOURCES

To learn more about trades in vehicle repair and maintenance, please visit **abdobooklinks.com** or scan this QR code. These links are routinely monitored and updated to provide the most current information available.

INDEX

associate's degrees, 52
automobile
   body and glass repairers, 12–13, 26, 29, 57
   diagnostics, 10, 21–22, 25, 48
   maintenance, 5, 9, 22, 25
   manufacturers, 8–9, 25, 52, 61
   mechanics/techs, 10–12, 21–22, 25, 52, 57
   repair shops, 10, 21
   repairs, 9–13, 21–22, 25–26, 29, 52

batteries, 14, 25, 33, 38, 41
bead breakers, 13, 30
Benz, Karl, 8
Benz Patent-Motorwagen, 8
bicycles
   assembly, 34
   mechanics, 14–15, 34, 37, 48, 52, 57
   repair stands, 14
   repairs, 8, 14, 34, 37, 46
   shops, 8, 34, 37, 48, 52–53
   tune-ups, 34
bike tire project, 50–51

certifications, 52, 54
chain tools, 14
chain whips, 14
cleaning, 12, 15, 30, 34, 38, 41, 48, 53
creepers, 10
crimping tools, 11

dents, 12–13, 26
diagnostic software tools, 10, 21, 25, 30
diesel vehicles, *see* automobiles
documentation, 25
dynamometers, 13, 30

edge pliers, 13
education, 5, 47, 52, 54
electrical systems, 18, 33, 41, 57
electronic control units (ECUs), 10

engines, 5, 7–9, 12–13, 15, 18, 21–22, 25, 33, 38, 41, 44, 52, 54, 57, 61
   diesel, 21
   internal combustion, 8, 21
   steam, 7
estimate write-ups, 25–26

finances, 58–59
Ford, Henry, 9
fuel systems, 30, 33, 41

glue tabs, 12

hose removal, 15

inventory, 37

job search tips, 53

knockdowns, 12–13

Lawson, Harry, 7
lights, 11, 19, 22
lockrings, 14, 51

marine vehicles
   maintenance, 5, 38, 52
   manufacturers, 38
   marinas, 38, 53, 61
   propellers, 41
   repairs, 41
   techs, 15, 38, 41, 57
Maxwell, John, 55
Model T, 9
Motorcycle Mechanics Institute, 52
motorcycles
   maintenance, 5, 30, 33
   mechanics/techs, 13–14, 30, 33, 52, 57
   repairs, 30
   tune-ups, 30
   upgrades/modifications, 33
multimeters, 14, 33

National Institute for Automotive Service Excellence, 52

oil changes, 15, 22, 38

painting, 29
pans, 11, 22
parts washers, 12
"penny farthing," 7
pneumatic dent pullers, 12
polishing, 13, 29

safety, 7–8, 14–15, 22, 29, 34, 54
salary ranges, 57
sanding, 29, 41
Savery, Thomas, 7
screwdrivers, 13
self-employment, 57–58
semitrucks, 8, 21
skills, 5, 17–19, 21, 46, 48, 52, 57
soldering irons, 15
suspension, 25, 33–34, 37, 57

tire irons, 13, 30
tire pumps, 14–15
tires, 11, 13, 15, 22, 30, 34, 37
   repairs, 30, 37
   replacements, 22, 30, 37
   rotations, 22
training, 5, 44, 52–54, 61
transmissions, 12, 22, 25, 57

US Bureau of Labor Statistics, 57

vehicle fluids, 11, 15, 17–18, 22, 30
vehicle lifts, 10
vision board, 42–43
von Drais, Karl, 7

welding, 29
Winton, Alexander, 8
wire brushes, 15
wrenches, 11, 13–14